CW01086404

I SPY

WITH MY LITTLE EYE

OCCUPATIONS

Copyright © 2021
All rights reserved. No part of this publication may be reproduced, distributed, or transmitted in any form or by any means, including photocopying, recording, or other electronic or mechanical methods, without the prior written permission of the publisher.

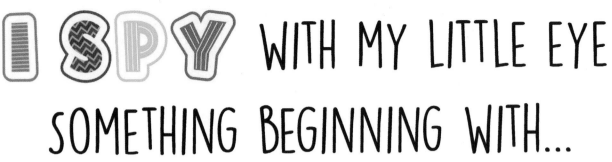

I SPY WITH MY LITTLE EYE SOMETHING BEGINNING WITH...

A IS FOR

ARCHITECT

I SPY WITH MY LITTLE EYE SOMETHING BEGINNING WITH...

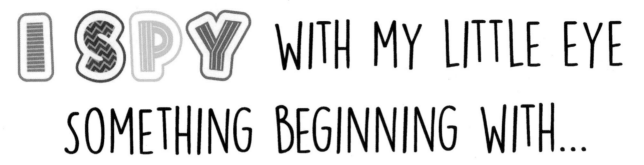

B IS FOR

BAKER

I SPY WITH MY LITTLE EYE SOMETHING BEGINNING WITH...

G

IS FOR

CLOWN

I SPY WITH MY LITTLE EYE SOMETHING BEGINNING WITH...

D IS FOR

DOCTOR

 WITH MY LITTLE EYE
SOMETHING BEGINNING WITH...

E  IS FOR

I SPY WITH MY LITTLE EYE SOMETHING BEGINNING WITH...

IS FOR

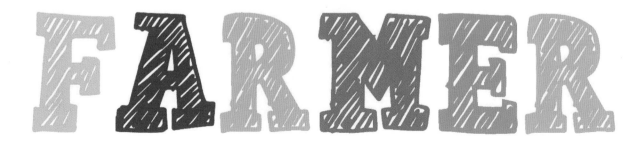

FARMER

I SPY WITH MY LITTLE EYE SOMETHING BEGINNING WITH...

H IS FOR

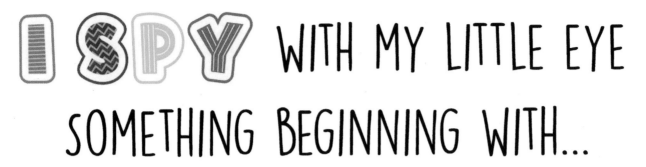

I SPY WITH MY LITTLE EYE SOMETHING BEGINNING WITH...

 IS FOR

 Hello

 你好

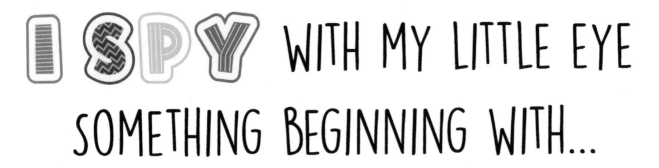

I SPY WITH MY LITTLE EYE SOMETHING BEGINNING WITH...

J IS FOR

JUDGE

I SPY WITH MY LITTLE EYE SOMETHING BEGINNING WITH...

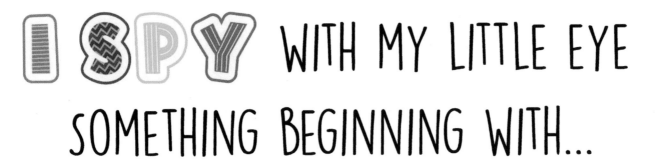

L IS FOR

LIFEGUARD

I SPY WITH MY LITTLE EYE SOMETHING BEGINNING WITH... M

M IS FOR

MUSICIAN

I SPY WITH MY LITTLE EYE SOMETHING BEGINNING WITH...

N IS FOR

NURSE

I SPY WITH MY LITTLE EYE SOMETHING BEGINNING WITH...

O IS FOR

OCEANOGRAPHER

I SPY WITH MY LITTLE EYE SOMETHING BEGINNING WITH...

P IS FOR

PAINTER

I SPY WITH MY LITTLE EYE SOMETHING BEGINNING WITH...

P IS FOR

PILOT

I SPY WITH MY LITTLE EYE SOMETHING BEGINNING WITH...

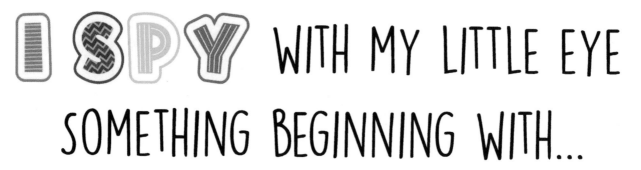

S IS FOR SCIENTIST

I SPY WITH MY LITTLE EYE SOMETHING BEGINNING WITH...

T IS FOR TEACHER

I SPY WITH MY LITTLE EYE SOMETHING BEGINNING WITH...

I SPY WITH MY LITTLE EYE SOMETHING BEGINNING WITH...

Printed in Great Britain
by Amazon

56783858R00025